EDINBURGH

FRAME *by* FRAME

WAVERLEY Station - built in 1868 by the North British Railway Company - and Princes Street Gardens are at the heart of Edinburgh, along with the castle that looms over them.

They are all still at its centre today and not that much has changed since the 19th century.

But in the days of the steam trains, the soot blackened all the buildings in the vicinity. These included the Church of Scotland's forbidding General Assembly building and the National Gallery, with its classical columns, all of it contributing to the city's reputation as Auld Reekie.

Some, however, nostalgically remember those days, when the streets were largely empty of traffic.

It was a time when children could safely run from one side of Waverley Bridge to the other, waving at the driver, hoping he would sound his whistle with a great, wheezy, "Woop, woop," and a puff of smoke before disappearing into the tunnel.

The gardens, created when the stinking Nor Loch was drained back in the 18th century, were originally private, with dogs, cricket, perambulators and smoking all forbidden.

Meanwhile, people who wanted to enter with bath chairs, had to present a doctor's certificate to the Garden Committee to prove their illness was not contagious.

Once the gardens were taken over by the council, they became - and in many ways still are - a green lung, where Edinburgh's residents could relax, play putting, buy ice-cream or simply sit under the trees.

They might also have listened to a band performing in the Ross Bandstand. First built in 1877, the current bandstand and seating area were developed in the 1930s and still play a vital part in the Edinburgh Festival and Hogmanay celebrations.

Editor: Joan Burnie
Picture Research: Brian Gallagher, Ann-Marie Nimmo
Design & Production: Bill Sullivan
Marketing & Circulation: Debbie Ramsay, Tom Heffernan

ISBN 0-9544202-8-4

It's all fun and games

Playing the likes of leapfrog was popular and kids spent much more time outdoors than their modern counterparts do

Jumping into action
Schoolkids play together in the playground in Morningside. No trainers but sensible laced-up shoes and boots and, of course, short trousers for the boys

Making a splash
Portobello outdoor swimming pool busy with bathers in April 1955

WE were a lot hardier back in the 30s and the immediate post-World War II days, when swimming pools were outside and generally unheated.

Portobello Bathing Pool, until the indoor Commonwealth Pool was opened in 1970, was by far the largest in Edinburgh. It boasted a wave machine, diving boards and tiers of concrete seats for hundreds of spectators to watch its beauty contests and swimming galas or merely to make sure wee Jimmy didn't get out of his depth.

There were, however, no bikinis.

Back then, kids costumes were often knitted for them by their grannies – with occasional unfortunate results, as wool is not the most buoyant of fabrics.

Designer fashion and foreign holidays were still some way off for the masses.

There were no cheap flights or package holidays to Spain.

Families instead made a whole day of it at Portobello. They flocked there in the early morning and stayed until it was time to go home for tea, carrying their own "pieces" with them for lunch and a "chittering bite" after their swim.

By the 60s, things were, if not exactly swinging among the general population, certainly changing as people began looking outwards and wanted more from their free time than a wave machine and a day at Portobello.

Even a day at the zoo with its exotic animals was no substitute for going abroad, especially now that there was this distinct, strange new tribe who appeared to have arrived almost overnight – teenagers.

Adults were not sure how to treat these almost alien creatures with their longer hair, their clothes and their pop music.

They no longer looked, behaved or dressed as previous generations had, like younger versions of their parents. They wanted to live the kind of life they saw not just in the cinema but increasingly on the telly, which was rapidly replacing the radio and becoming commonplace within their homes.

Edinburgh certainly had its rockers but was more of a mod town with that fashionable import from Italy, the scooter, becoming almost as desirable as its ice-cream.

It may have been the era that brought us The Beatles and The Rolling Stones, however, it was still a fairly innocent time – Let's Spend The Night Together by the Stones was banned by Auntie Beeb.

The best or the worst, the internet, iPods, tablets and mobile phones were yet to come for this generation but the times they were a' changing, even in douce old Edinburgh.

Pool's winners
Claire and Frank Thomson, below, get free season tickets for being first in the pool and bottom, two youngsters take the plunge

Class action A university student looks the worse for wear after taking part in the traditional battle between rival candidates for the rectorship

Get a kick out of it These children were among thousands who played football in the city's recreation grounds in 1946

Muddy marvellous Edinburgh Amazons take on the Varsity Maidens at Women's Sevens in April 1962. As one of the players scores a try on The Meadows, some of their fellow students take a keen interest in proceedings

Who's walking who? This five-year-old laddie is holding tight to his Great Dane pet Sonka in Princes Street Gardens in May 1940

▲ **Join the club** Grand Golf Tournament, Leith Links, May 17, 1867. Players included A Strath, David Park, Bob Kirk, James Anderson, Jamie Dunn, William Dow, Willie Dunn, Alexander Greig, Tom Morris, Tom Morris Jnr and George Morris

lonumental view erseas visitors look t at the city from the ott Monument in 71

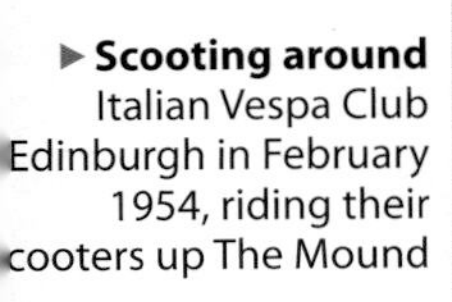

▶ **Scooting around** Italian Vespa Club Edinburgh in February 1954, riding their cooters up The Mound

▲ **Smiles on the Mile**
Kids messing around on the High Street next to St Giles Cathedral, on the Royal Mile, in 1954

▶ **Ring leaders** Royston Primary School youngsters play in their electrically heated swimming pool in the assembly hall. Allan Triplett, six, is pictured with a rubber ring in December 1968

▼ **Tu-tu ticket collector** Ballerina Patricia Merrin takes tickets from passengers on the train. She was part of the entertainment when British Rail gave their high-speed London to Edinburgh express train a trial run in Scotland in April 1978

School trip
A rather stern-looking teacher takes her pupils along the street in the city's west end in 1954

▲ **Sporting set**
Tennis player Ted Slawek at Murrayfield in May 1954

◀ **Medal winners**
Ian Stewart and Ian McCafferty after taking gold and silver in the 5000m race in the July 197 Commonwealth Games

▲ **Good luck message**
The Scottish swimming team ready for the 1970 Commonwealth Games at Meadowbank Stadium

▶ **Day at the castle**
Schoolchildren have a ball as adults take in the views from the lofty landmark

◄ **Penguin Parade**
Tuxedo the king penguin at Edinburgh's Napier College of Commerce and Technology, visiting the students who adopted him in November 1978

▲ **Funky fashions**
A selection of way-out cats on Rose Street in the 70s

Courts in the act
Kids playing at the back of a tenement block in 1970

City makes the outdoors great

People flocked to put the broad streets and green spaces to a wide range of uses – both serious and recreational

Votes for women
Suffragettes march down Princes Street in 1909 led by Flora Drummond and Emmeline Pankhurst

ANTLES

PRINCES Street, the capital's main thoroughfare, with the gardens on one side and shops on the other, could have been deliberately created for parades and protest.

From the Suffragettes, in their buttoned boots and sweeping skirts at the beginning of the 20th century, to protesters against the Iraq War at the start of the 21st, they've all marched, walked and driven along it.

For politicians, pipers and performers at the Edinburgh Festival, its broad mile becomes an outdoor theatre and on Hogmanay, when the street is closed to all traffic, it is where everyone from the city itself and from further afield, congregates to welcome in the brand new year.

The famous gardens, with the war memorial, statues, winding paths and bandstand, are divided by the National Galleries of Art.

It is the place where office workers spill out to sit and eat their lunch on the grass and children play tig or hide and seek among the bushes before paddling in the recently restored Ross Fountain.

That was not something which was encouraged back in the days when children were seen rather than heard and forbidden to run around the gardens by the omnipotent parkies with their whistles, who ensured the immaculate lawns were never walked on.

Beside the steps in north-east corner is the oldest floral clock in the world, created back in 1903 by the then superintendent of parks, the splendidly named, John McHattie, in honour of King Edward VII's coronation. Ever since, the clock is replanted each year in spring to celebrate a different event or anniversary, from the Commonwealth Games to the Queen's Diamond Jubilee.

But Edinburgh has many more green spaces that are well used by residents and visitors for rest and recreation.

Holyrood Park, home to Holyrood Palace, sweeps up to the extinct volcano, Arthur's Seat, and includes Salisbury Crags, the steep, jagged cliff where crime writer Ian Rankin dumped a body in one of his Rebus books.

The fictional Rebus himself lives near The Meadows.

The 1886 International Exhibition of Industry, Science and Art was held there and the whalebone arch over Jawbone Walk is a relic of the event, taken from a stand run by the Shetland and Fair Isle Knitters.

It is also where Hearts and Hibs began playing their football and where the first derby between the two teams took place in 1875.

Football is still a fixture in the park – for amateur teams or just for kids who want somewhere to kick a ball, although these days there are almost as many skateboarders and bikers flying along its paths, dodging the joggers.

Far more decorous are the Royal Botanic Gardens in which ball games are still forbidden and whose lily pond is also home to some of the most vicious swans known to visitors – and especially to any child who gets too close.

The animals, at Edinburgh Zoo along the road in Corstorphine, are safely behind bars – although the daily penguin parade remains a highlight, even if they have been slightly usurped as the main attraction by the recently arrived pandas.

Should Tian Tian and Yang Guang have a cub, Edinburgh will have yet another reason to celebrate.

◄ **Tartan parade**
Scottish ladies team at the opening ceremony of the Commonwealth Games in 1970

▼ **Landmark**
The majestic Arthur's Seat, an extinct volcano, dominates Holyrood Park

Following the tune
roud pipe bands are
enned in by massive
rowds on Princes Street
August 1951

Flower power
Floral clock display for the Festival of Britain in 1951

Constitutional
Coronation Walk at The Meadows with whalebone arch at the entrance

▲ **Oasis of calm**
The Royal Botanic Gardens where a mother and two children and office workers spend a lunch hour, in 1955

▶ **Heavy brigade**
Chieftain tanks of the Royal Scots Dragoon Guards drive down Princes Street to mark the regiment's 300th anniversary

▶ **Sunset on Leith**
A Park and Ride boat heads into Edinburgh in October 1997

▶ **Big brother is watching**
The penguins at Edinburgh Zoo can't believe their eyes as they face up to the new arrival of a queen-sized penguin. But the new family member is not for real – young actress Mary McCusker changed into the costume to get some real-life experience for the show Flibberty and the Penguin in January 1974

◀ **Yes men**
Donald Dewar, George Robertson and John Home Robertson standing outside the Royal High School Assembly building in Edinburgh while campaigning for the Yes vote in devolution referendum

▽ **Dog day afternoon**
Princes Street Gardens with a man walking a dog in 1939

Royal mission
Sir Francis Grant on the way to read a proclamation at the Mercat Cross

Wild city
An aerial view of Edinburgh Zoo taken in 1914

Out and about
A woman pushes a pram under the whale's jawbone arch that forms the entrance to The Meadows

▸ **Election fever**
SNP candidate Willie Wolfe's election campaign cavalcade hits the streets in a Hillman Sunbeam while Labour supporters heckle

▾ **Coats and tails**
Horsedrawn coaches during Horseman's Sunday Service at Queen's Park

▸ **Soldiers on parade**
The King's Own Scottish Borderers marching through Edinburgh in regimental colours

Shadow of war During the ARP World War II Home Front air defence rehearsals in Edinburgh, a little girl finds herself on the wrong side of the wooden barricade as others look on

Lifestyle changes down the decades

Many of its buildings have stood for centuries but the people who have made Edinburgh their home have always reflected the fashions of the times

▲ Bumpy ride
The cobbled street of Gill Place in 1955

UNLIKE many other cities, Edinburgh has not changed an enormous amount during its long history.

The high tenements and closes of the medieval Old Town remain, with the Royal Mile stretching between the Castle and the Palace of Holyroodhouse – down which Bonny Prince Charlie and his Jacobite army swept.

The Old Town slums are now a thing of the past but many of the more impressive buildings remain, including John Knox House, which still stands just down the road from St Giles Cathedral.

The cobbled streets once frequented by world-famous writers Sir Walter Scott, Sir Arthur Conan Doyle and Robert Louis Stevenson are all still there. Now they are popular with modern day authors including Ian Rankin and Alexander McCall Smith.

The Georgian New Town was built between 1765 and 1850, boasting broad avenues and splendid architecture.

The old lady of Princes Street, Jenners – the capital's equivalent of London's Harrods, has changed owners down the years but still dominates the east end of Princes Street.

The Railway hotel The North British opened at 1 Princes Street on October 15, 1902.

It was rechristened The Balmoral in the 1980s. The clock on its tower continues to be set a few minutes fast so those hurrying to Waverley will not miss their train as they run down the steps to the station.

But although much appears the same, it would be wrong to assume that Edinburgh is frozen in aspic.

These archive photographs show us how its citizens have gradually changed over the years, even if the spectacular backdrop in which they live, shop and stroll, stays much the same.

This evolution is no less fascinating and interesting than the more conventional history we learn at school about our capital's famous sons and daughters.

So we can see the cars our grandparents drove, laugh at the clothes they wore and understand a little more about the way in which those who'll never have a plaque erected outside their house spent their working lives and leisure time.

We can catch a glimpse of Edinburgh at war and the city once again at peace, at a time when the flat cap was as much a part of a man's uniform as a careful perm was for his wife and when our policemen wore pointy helmets.

The children have perhaps changed the most. Most young girls these days prefer jeans and trainers to their best dresses and sandals when they have a day out. And no modern boy would be seen dead in those hand-knitted jumpers and short baggy breeks.

Through the pictures, we can, with the next Commonwealth Games almost upon us, be reminded of when they came – twice – to Edinburgh. And how the Coronation was celebrated in red, white and blue in 1953 at a time when the only Parliament was at Westminster and devolution was not even on the political horizon.

▲ Swift tailor
American Professor Dean Walker told the Edinburgh City Business Club that he had a hard time trying to buy a shirt in Scotland. After explaining exactly what he had in mind, he was handed a ready-made shirt in 1935

Festive fun
ıthy Cameron, five, of
ıontgomery Street, plays
princess at a Christmas
ɑrty held in a Church
f Scotland hall

Window shopping
Fashions of the past in a Jenners window display

Poetry in motion
A memorial plate marking where Sir Walter Scott and Robert Burns met in 1786-1787, is unveiled at 7 Braid Place. Members of the Scott Club and Burns Federation attended the ceremony. Walter T Watson K.C. unveiled the memorial tablet in 1927

▲ **Loving it** These Edinburgh lasses were in a romantic mood on Valentine's Day 1951

◄ **Shop boy** St Mirren football player Archie Buchanan in his Edinburgh shop in 1969

► **Long way down** Waverley steps in 1948. Today, escalators make the descent and climb easier

Stitches in time Janet Rumbles, of Stenhouse Avenue, Edinburgh, won the National Sewing Competition. She is pictured working on a creation at her school in May 1953

arly starters These children were all born ematurely and thrived thanks to the dedication of ctors and nurses in the first vital days. The kids were ed for in the intensive care unit of Simpson Memorial ternity Pavilion in Edinburgh

Signs of industry wo new coaling cranes arrived t Leith Docks in 1933

Buying in a bygone era
Shoppers go about their business in Kirkgate, in 1923

Time for work The west end of Princes Street in July 1948, where trams are soon to make a comeback

◀ **Day out of note** Schoolgirls arrive at the Usher Hall for a concert being given by the Scottish National Orchestra in 1953

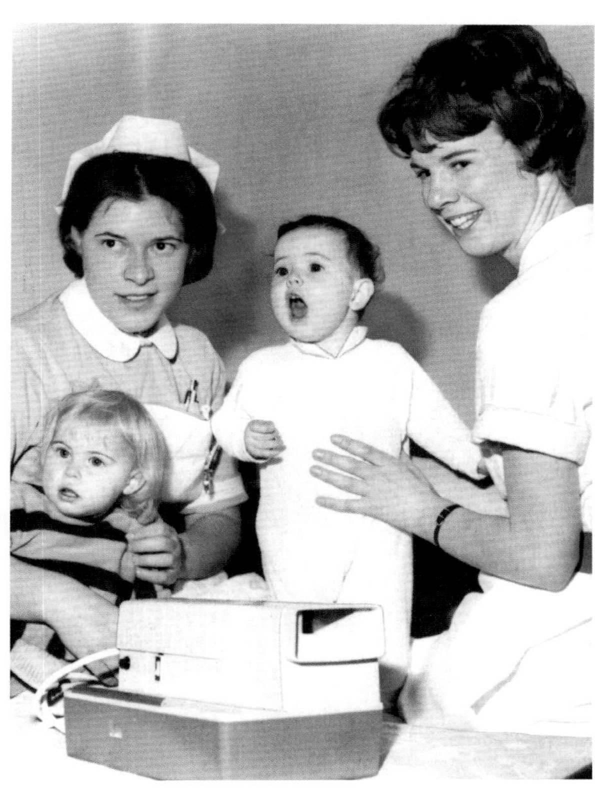

▶ **Innovation** Student nurse Sylvia Glass and physiotherapist Anne Fraser treat cystic fibrosis sufferers Tracy and Anne with a new humidifier at the Royal Hospital for Sick Children in 1968. The hospital opened on February 15, 1860

Clearing out Men bag up rubbish in the back court of Begg's Buildings, Abbeyhill, in September 1958, watched by a crowd of youngsters

◄ **Simple pleasures** Duncan Cameron feeds the pigeons in the Grassmarket in the 50s – where the city gallows once stood

◄ **Any colour you like** A stream of uniformly black cars

► **Watching you** A TV detector van in 1967

▲ **Bright idea** A new lighting system comes into effect in Princes Street in 1968

► **Royal replica** Jenners on Princes Street put this exact replica of Princess Diana's wedding dress on show on July 30, 1981. It was copied by designers Manouche in their London workshop and was on sale for £295

▼ **Bombed** The ruins of a bonded warehouse that was attacked beside the Water of Leith, in the 40s

▼ **Majestic** Regent Terrace, designed by William Playfair. Today the street is home to the US Consulate and the French Consul-General

▶ **Famous residents** Charlotte Square, which was home to antiseptic pioneer Joseph Lister. Field Marshal Douglas Haig was also born there

▼ **Story time** Matron Isobel Baird reading to some children in 1967

▲ **Looking back** St Andrew Street, Leith, back view in June, 1949. The street has since been demolished

▲ **Keeping time** The North British Hotel clock tower captured in 1953. It first began ticking in 1902. It's now known as The Balmoral clock tower

▲ **Rainy day** One boy hides under a coat on a wet day in St Andrew Street, Leith, in June 1947

▼ **Hole lot of fundraising** Everyone knows what crocheting is – knitting a lot of holes together. But not everyone can do it. Florence Stein, however, was an expert and, just to prove it to the citizens of Edinburgh, she sat outside a shop keeping her needles busy. Florence, aged 60, had just retired as a district nurse on Arran, and spent 36 hours crocheting to raise funds for the charity Shelter on September 7,1970

If you want to know the way... A lost child talks to a policeman in St Patrick Square

In a jam Lothian Road traffic at the Tollcross junction, in 1962, shows that rush hour is nothing new

Strike day
A municipal busmen's strike over pay left everyone resorting to walking on Princes Street in the 70s

Style statement
C&A store on Princes Street, in 1936, the year that it opened

▲ **Washing day** One of the city's many tenement buildings with clothes – and nappies – hung out to dry

◀ **Just the tick**
Lothian Region
Transport bus o
Princes Street i
the 70s

▶ **Still going strong**
Jenners snapped in Edinburgh, in 1994. It was founded in 1838

Coronation Street
Cumberland Street with decorations in May 1953

▲ **Making a meal of it** Pupils at Gracemount Primary School sit down to school dinner in May 1971

▼ **Taking a stand** Men gathered around the Robert Burns monument where Constitution and Bernard Street meet in Leith, in June 1947. The statue still stands on the street

▲ **Royal history** Whitehorse Close, off the Royal Mile, was the site of a royal mews in the 16th century

▲ **Bustle** The west end of Princes Street, looking east at the turn of the 19th and 20th centuries

► **Everybody out** 100 squatters were evicted by Sheriff officers at 1 St John Street, off the Royal Mile, in February, 1947

Industrial strife and working life

Workers in the capital enjoyed mixed fortunes as some traditional industries came under pressure

▲ **Holding position**
Violence erupted in March 1984 as police and coal mine pickets clashed at Bilston Glen pit near Edinburgh

Peer group
The election of two new peers at the Palace of Holyroodhouse in January 1941. The Earl of Mar and Kelly, who presided, is seen sitting behind the mace

EDINBURGH'S principal industries in the 21st century are tourism and, despite the catastrophic economic crash, banking.

The City's reputation as the UK's second largest financial centre after London may have taken a severe knock as a result but it is still, as it has always been since the Bank of Scotland was founded in 1695, a considerable employer.

But other industries, such as the once major one of brewing have more or less vanished.

Once, the capital was home to 35 different breweries, spewing out plumes of smoke from their coal and wood-burning boilers and merrily contributing to Edinburgh's nickname of Auld Reekie.

The largest and most successful were the William Younger Company, who began operating in Leith around 1750, and William McEwan, who, 100 years later, started up the Fountain Brewery, only half a mile away from Princes Street.

Sean Connery, who was born in the area, would have been familiar with the fumes and smell which permeated not just the adjacent streets but the entire city centre.

The companies eventually merged but all production ceased in the 1990s and the whole Fountainbridge site, which stretched over many acres, is now given over to modern offices.

We may not think of Edinburgh as somewhere where the heavier industries flourished but, until fairly recently, it supported both coal mining and shipbuilding.

The former was killed off following the bitter year-long 1984 Miners' Strike, which divided families and set brother against brother, and where police and the miners engaged in hand-to-hand fighting.

Old King Coal is now officially dead.

Miners no longer spill up and out from the cages and into the washrooms and showers after their back-breaking, grimy shifts underground.

The collieries and close knit mining communities that once ringed Edinburgh, including Bilston Glen and The Lady Victoria at Newtongrange, are now no more.

The latter is now a museum where schoolchildren come to learn about something that, within living memory, has become just another part of the tourist trade and the capital's long history.

Much the same has happened to shipbuilding down at Leith on the Forth, which, even if it never rivalled that of the Clyde's, was once a vibrant industry that echoed to the sound of riveters and the banging of the shipwrights.

All that is gone, like the colourful fisherwives who used to walk into town in their traditional wide petticoats with huge baskets on their backs to sell their wares in Edinburgh's main streets.

The cranes have been dismantled and the warehouses have been turned into smart flats.

The Royal Yacht Britannia, now permanently moored at Leith, and the cruise liners that dock down at the old wharfs are about all that is left of Edinburgh's maritime past.

The city also once had a huge publishing business, turning out more Bibles than any other part of the country.

Although companies such as Canongate and Luath still produce books, it is now more of a cottage industry.

But Edinburgh gave the world Conan Doyle's Sherlock Holmes and Robert Louis Stevenson along with today's Ian Rankin and Alexander McCall Smith, as well as the UK's biggest Book Festival in Charlotte Square.

It is therefore rightly recognised and honoured by UNICEF as its first chosen City of Literature.

▼ **Sweetie wife**
Duncans of Edinburgh worker Rena Monaghan holds a tray of chocolates with granddaughter Nicola on her knee in 1988

▲ **Chocs away**
Dr John McKay, Lord Provost, and Bob Baxter, of Duncans of Edinburgh, tasting chocolate

◄ **The sweet life**
Workers at the famous Duncans chocolate factory in Edinburgh, a long-established local firm who later merged with Rowntrees

▼ **Business woman**
Sheila Watt, pictured in 1964, was an accountant in the new ladies-only bank, the National Commercial Bank of Scotland, which opened in Edinburgh

Brewers troop
Scottish and Newcastle workers on a protest march in Princes Street

Getting wired in
Girls at work wire-stitchin copies of the Scottish edition of the National Service Guide, which was printed and produced in Edinburgh in 1939

Cash call
Model Ray Reid was pictured using the first Royal Bank of Scotland cash dispensing machine at the West End branch on December 28, 1967

Watching brief
Portobello Power Station in December 1951, with shift control engineer J S Arrighi checking the vital needles

▶ **Carry that weight**
Fishwife Mrs Liston, of Newhaven, pictured in May, 1955, carrying her basket on her back with a support strap on her forehead

◀ **Kitchen cabinet**
Gordon Baxter with daughter Audrey at famous soup company Baxters retail outlet in Rose Street

▼ **Angry words**
During the coal miners' dispute in March 1984, picket line violence flared at Bilston Glen pit, near Edinburgh, where pitmen were stoned and spat on

Getting the brush-off
Coal miners Danny Devine and Alex Kennedy (the naked one) get a wash and brush up after finishing a shift in 1986

Sew far, so good
Labourer Alan Howse put down his pick and shovel and reached for a needle and thread. He became a star at Edinburgh's Sewing School in Howe Street, the only man in a class of girls. Alan, 23, was pictured in April, 1975 making a jacket to save money

He made all the pies
Baker Thomas Hogg, seen in February 1957, was kept busy with football matches at Tynecastle and Easter Road and a rugby match at Murrayfield

▸ **Happy ending**
Miner John Millar, pictured in March, 1974, was glad to be back at Monktonhall Colliery after dispute

▾ **Going underground**
Pit props are hammered into position under the steel roof supports at Whitehill Colliery. It was owned by the Lothian Coal Company – specialists in colliery efficiency and pioneers of the modern system of intensive, fully mechanised mining

▸ **Caught on film**
A shellfish vendor pictured in April 1924 at the Lawnmarket

The many faces of Auld Reekie

Stunning landmarks illustrate the continuous development of a city that reflected the changing times

City of spires
The spectacular view over the capital from Calton Hill in 1950

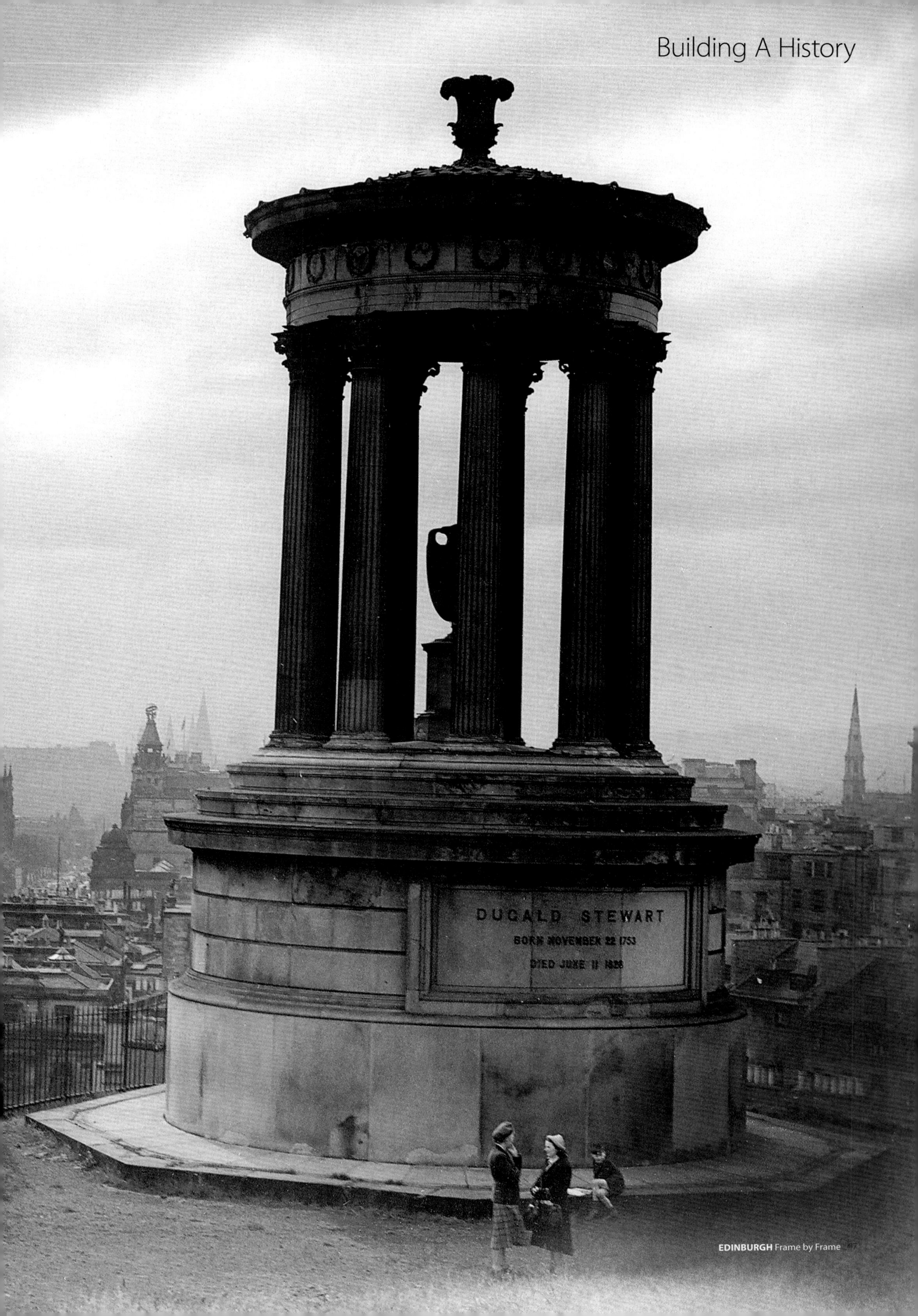
DUGALD STEWART
BORN NOVEMBER 22 1753
DIED JUNE 11 1828

▼ View to a thrill Calton Hill, St Andrew's House and the Old Castle Gaol as they were pictured in 1964

▲ Heritage An image of Saughton Hall, now demolished

THE best way to see the city is by walking, and anyone strolling – however briefly – around the capital would not find it difficult to understand why Edinburgh's Old and New Towns were both named in 1995 by UNESCO as World Heritage Sites.

Both these contrasting parts of the capital, with the medieval houses on one side of Princes Street and the neo-classical Georgian on the other, underline Edinburgh's international significance and give the city its unique character.

History is around every corner, down its old cobbled streets and built into its grey stones.

The capital has it all, with around 5000 listed buildings in an architectural pick 'n' mix that has been formed over nine centuries.

Although there have been inevitable losses, including one of the finest examples of 17th century domestic architecture, Saughton Hall, which was damaged by fire in the 1920s and subsequently demolished, Edinburgh has largely escaped the worst excesses of redevelopment.

Our pictures may be old but, apart from the ancient cars and general lack of traffic in the streets, they don't look all that different from that which we see today.

Those who climb up Calton Hill, with its observatory, colonnaded folly and Nelson's Monument built to commemorate his victory in the Battle of Trafalgar in 1805, will be rewarded with a glorious panoramic view of the city beneath.

And if they are there at 1pm, they will not only hear the gun fire from the ramparts of the Castle but watch as the Time Ball falls down from the monument's centre.

Edinburgh is, of course, not only full of listed buildings but also of memorials to the once famous and renowned.

The most prominent example is that dedicated to Sir Walter Scott.

Built thanks to public subscription, in florid Victorian Gothic style on Princes Street, the tourists who troop up its 287 steps will also be able to see much of the capital laid out before them.

The oldest building in Edinburgh is thought to be St Margaret's Chapel within the Castle walls.

This is where the Saxon princess worshipped after she married Scotland's King Malcolm III.

The newest is the Parliament at the bottom of the Royal Mile, which was formally opened by the Queen in 2004. But the Old Parliament, in which Scotland's politicians met until the Union of the Crowns in 1707, still stands behind the High Kirk of St Giles where, in 1637, one Jennie Geddes, a market trader, reputably threw her stool at the minister when he attempted to preach from the Anglican Book of Common Prayer.

Scotland's people and church stuck fast to the protestant creed as decreed by John Knox, whose own house still stands – a stone's, or possibly stool's throw, away from St Giles.

The Old Parliament became the home of Scotland's Supreme Court and the old debating chamber became Advocates Hall, where lawyers in their wigs pace up and down with their clients.

St Andrew Square and Charlotte Square guard each end of George Street, Edinburgh's principal shopping centre after Princes Street.

When they were first constructed in the 18th century, both squares, with their private gardens, swiftly became the favoured residential area for the gentry.

They rapidly moved down from the no-longer fashionable Old Town into the cleaner, broader streets of the New Town.

Henry Dundas, 1st Viscount Melville, who still stands high up on his tall pillar, dominating not only St Andrew Square but the skyline, lived at No36 in Dundas House.

A hundred years later, it was to become the headquarters of the Royal Bank Of Scotland, as the residents moved out and the squares became the capital's main commercial and financial centres.

St Andrew Square once claimed to be the richest area in the whole of Scotland. With Harvey Nichols department store along with various designer shops such as Louis Vuitton now occupying much of its east side, perhaps it can be called that again.

▼ Historic
Nelson's Monument, dedicated to the hero of Trafalgar, stands proudly on Calton Hill

Taking wing
An aerial view with a Cessna plane flying over the city in 1969

▶ City church
St Giles Cathedral, pictured in 1950, is also known as the High Kirk of Edinburgh

Remembrance
The Royal Scots Memorial in Princes Street Gardens

▼ **Historic home**
The Leith house of Mary of Guise, Mother of Mary Queen of Scots, pictured in 1947

▲ **Royal apartments**
The spectacular Palace of Holyroodhouse is the Queen's official residence in Scotland

▶ **Splendour**
An aerial view of Holyrood Palace overlooked by Arthur's Seat, taken in 1950

▲ **Seat of power**
St Andrew's House pictured here in 1950, former home to the Scottish Government

◄ **Atmospheric**
The Great Hall in the old Parliament House, which was home to the pre-Union parliament

▼ **High grade**
An aerial view of Princes Street in 1963

▲ **Dizzy heights** The view down Advocate's Close, where children happily played and with the Scott Monument looming large in the background

▼ Changes
The Tolbooth in the Canongate, a former jail and courthouse and now the People's Story Museum

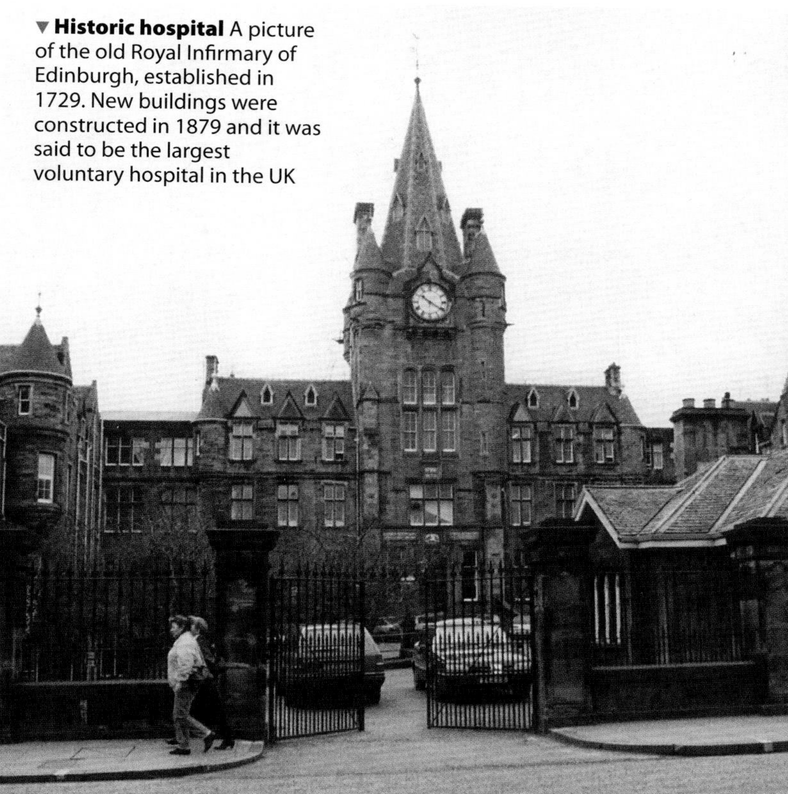

▼ Historic hospital A picture of the old Royal Infirmary of Edinburgh, established in 1729. New buildings were constructed in 1879 and it was said to be the largest voluntary hospital in the UK

◄ Built to last
St Margaret's Chapel, in Edinburgh Castle, is the oldest surviving building in the city. It was built in the 12th century and restored in the 19th century

▼ Indestructible
Edinburgh Castle dominates the city skyline and reflects more than 1000 years of history. The volcanic rock which forms its base gives the castle its unique defensive position – one that has stood the test of time. The city of Edinburgh itself grew outward from the rock

When a city went off to battle

The capital has always taken pride in its Armed Forces and its servicemen and women have done the country proud

▲ **On the march**
Onlookers climb on to railings to get a glimpse of soldiers of the Gordon Highlanders marching through Edinburgh

The real Dad's Army
The Home Guard at their stand-down parade in Princes Street in December 1944

EDINBURGH has been a military town for hundreds of years. The sheer rock and extinct volcano on which David I built the castle in the 12th century, served as a base for his army and a royal palace and continued to do so for another 500 years.

It was said that whoever held the castle, held Scotland.

In the late 13th century, the castle was under almost constant siege from England's King Edward I as he fought to seize the then vacant Scottish throne before being sent home to think again.

It was attacked by the English army again in 1571 in an attempt to capture Mary, Queen of Scots and a century later Oliver Cromwell succeeded.

It was still in English hands when Bonnie Prince Charlie marched his troops into Edinburgh and down the Royal Mile but he and his Highlanders failed to retake it.

For years, it was also used as a military prison but, in 1814, it was declared a national monument.

However, its connection with the military continues to this day as the home of the Scottish National War Memorial.

The Army's base in Edinburgh is now at Redford Barracks in the suburb of Colinton. Although the number of soldiers and regiments are greatly reduced these days, the capital still takes pride in the Armed Forces.

During World War II, it was used as a training base not just for British soldiers but also for that exotic breed, the GI, who brought the jitterbug and, most prized of all and much to the delight of the women folk, nylons to the capital.

But arguably, the Edinburgh servicemen who contributed most to the war effort were those of the city's 603 Air Force Squadron.

Initially, it was just part of the Auxiliary Air Force, created by volunteers in the 1920s, which as the Second World War threatened, turned itself from an amateur weekend flyers' outfit into the best and bravest of the few who defeated the German Air Force in the Battle of Britain.

The 603 Squadron shot down more German planes than any other RAF unit.

However, it suffered many casualties – 13 pilots alone on the first day of the battle – and although Edinburgh itself largely escaped the bombing, more than 8000 of those who served in the Armed Forces lost their lives.

But eventually, after VE and VJ Days, the boys (and girls) came marching home to a tumultuous welcome and the inevitable parade down Princes Street.

But Edinburgh also has another, less celebrated, defence force – not just the Dad's Army, the Home Guard, but the Royal Company of Archers formed back in 1822.

They are the Monarch's official bodyguard in Scotland, on duty every summer during the annual Royal visit to Holyrood, when they march down to the Palace, preceded by the pipes and drums of their band and holding their unstrung bows in their right hands to provide the King or Queen's guard of honour.

Its members must be Scots or have strong Scottish connections and membership – which totals 530 – is by election.

It is also all male – and members pay an annual subscription of £25.

They accompany HM to ceremonies such as garden parties, investitures, to Scotland's ancient Order of the Thistle and at the granting of new colours to the Scottish regiments.

Their duties are strictly ceremonial – a man with an eagle feather in his cap and an unstrung bow is unlikely to save the sovereign from harm.

But they are a colourful part of Scotland's and Edinburgh's military past as well as its present.

▲ Time to tuck in
Two soldiers from the west of Scotland enjoy a meal at Waverley Station while on leave in January 1945

▲ Skirling
Two Gurkha soldiers playing the bagpipes at Edinburgh Castle, in May 1951

► It's that time again
Edinburgh Gunner Robert Thompson prepares the famous One O'Clock Gun for firing in 1945. The Gun is fired automatically by a nearby electric clock at 1pm every day (except Sunday) on the ramparts of Edinburgh Castle. It has done so since 1861. The tradition started in an effort to provide ships in the Firth of Forth with a time signal

▲ **Soldiers on parade**
HRH Princess Alice, Duchess of Gloucester, is pictured inspecting soldiers at Holyrood Palace

▶ **Celebration**
American servicemen carry a girl in Highland dance costume on their shoulders on Victory in Japan Day in August 1945

▼ **Bodyguards**
The High Constables and Guards of Honour at The Palace of Holyroodhouse were part of the Royal Household in Scotland

▼ Bowmen on parade
Members of the Royal Company of Archers, the King's bodyguard in Scotland, line up for inspection at the Palace of Holyroodhouse. They are wearing their distinctive uniforms including hats with feathers and ceremonial swords

▲ Homecoming
Private Robert Martin, from Glasgow, is welcomed arriving home on leave at Waverley Station in January 1945

▶ Respect
A large crowd watches a military ceremony at Arthur's Seat in Holyrood Park

▲ **Chocks away lads**
Captain Kennedy, chief flying instructor of the Edinburgh University Air Squadron, speaks to pupil pilots

▲ **Up and away**
Members of the Edinburgh University Air Squadron about to set off on training flights in 1954. The squadron was part of a national scheme to attract graduates into the Royal Air Force

City of cheer
Crowds gather to watch a pipe band marching down The Mound to celebrate Victory in Japan Day in August 1945

◀ **Stirring sounds**
The 52nd Lowland Division Pipe Band play in Princes Street Gardens in 1946

▲ **Remembrance**
The National War Memorial Service takes place within Edinburgh Castle

Darker side of a genteel city

Edinburgh may be celebrated for festivals and culture but its streets have also seen their share of trouble and played host to murderers including Burke and Hare

▲ **Black day** Eastern Cemetery in Edinburgh on November 22, 1960. Detectives walk towards a hearse carrying the body of John Wilson, who had been murdered. His murder was never solved

▼ Lock and key A prison van arrives at Saughton Prison in 1987

ALTHOUGH Edinburgh may not have quite the same reputation for gangsters and violence as the city at the opposite end of the M8, the capital has always had a darker side.

Not just the notorious brothel down in the douce Danube Street, which was run until the 70s by Dora Noyce, but its own gangs.

These days, they are largely based in the housing schemes on the outskirts. But 40 years ago, at weekends, the city centre became their battleground as teenage boys – and girls – fought hand to hand.

Things may be quieter these days but there is something about Edinburgh, especially at night and in the Old Town, which can send a shiver down most spines.

This was, after all, the home of the serial killers William Burke and William Hare, who murdered at least 16 people between 1827 and 1828 and sold their bodies to Edinburgh's Medical College for use in the doctors' anatomy classes.

Should you wander into the Grassmarket, just down from the Royal Mile, you might be tempted to have a drink in an old pub called The Last Drop, outside whose windows public hangings were held until 1864.

Even though the public hangings ended, judges up at the High Court would continue to tell condemned men and women they would: "Be hanged by the neck until dead" until the abolition of the death penalty in the 1960s.

The last woman to hear the words was Jessie King, convicted of killing two children in her care in 1889 and who was hung in Edinburgh's Calton Jail, now largely demolished – and on which St Andrew's House now stands.

The last Edinburgh man to suffer the ultimate punishment was George Robertson, who, in 1954, brutally stabbed to death his son and daughter and attempted to murder their mother.

Probably the most notorious killings of fairly recent times, in 1977, are what came to be known as the World's End Murders after the pub in which the victims, two 17-year-olds, called Christine Eadie and Helen Scott, were last seen alive. Angus Sinclair was acquitted of their murders 30 years later, although there are moves to retry him.

The Lothian and Borders Force that policed Edinburgh until the creation of Scotland's National Police Force, can be traced back to the 1680s, when a Town Guard was formed and earned a fearsome reputation as they forcibly exerted law and order as well as an 8pm curfew.

In 1805 Edinburgh City Police replaced the Town Guard. Meanwhile, Lothian and Borders Fire and Rescue Service – also now merged into a national force – was the first municipal brigade in the world, formed in 1824 after a series of disastrous fires in the capital.

With so many buildings so close together, fire was, and still is, a hazard. But Edinburgh is rightly proud of two services who served it well for more than 200 eventful years.

▲ Hero at work A firefighter tackling a house blaze at Queensferry Street Lane, in August 1998

▲ **Scene of the crime** In September 1930, master printer James McNair Dalgleish was shot and killed by Church of Scotland minister Reverend Peter Carmichael Marr. A verdict of insanity was returned at his trial and he was was ordered to be detained in strict custody "until His Majesty's Pleasure be known".

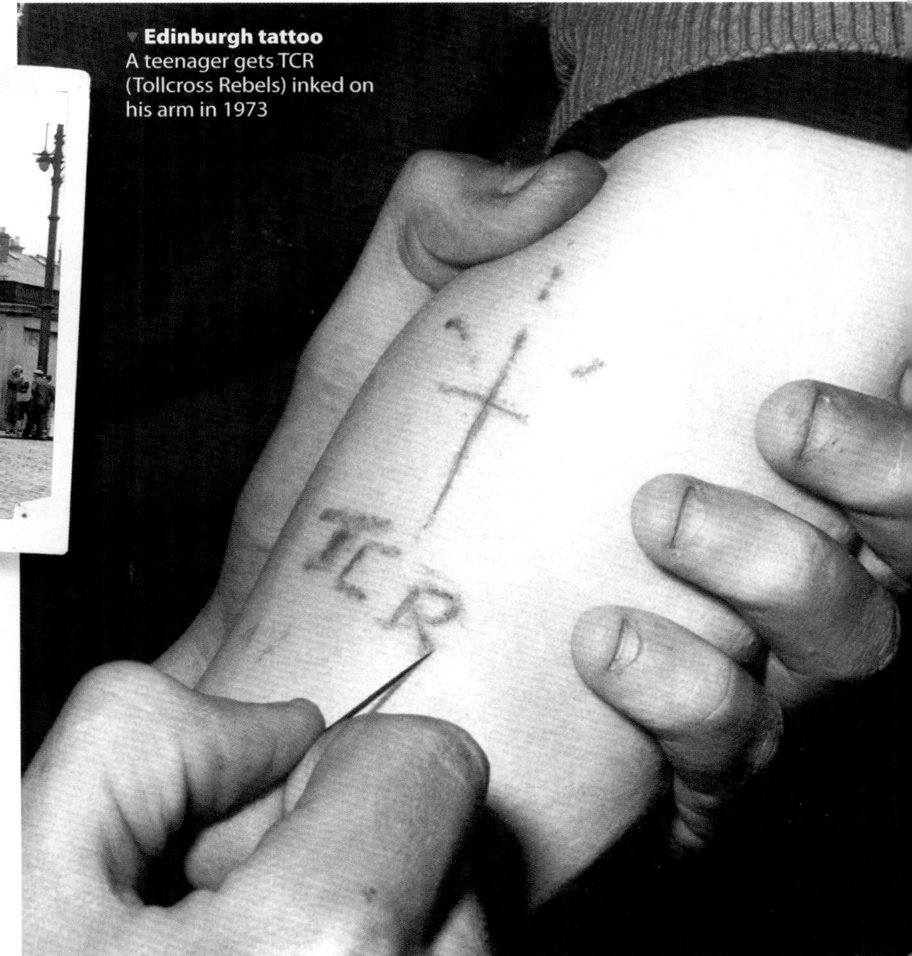

▼ **Edinburgh tattoo** A teenager gets TCR (Tollcross Rebels) inked on his arm in 1973

▼ **Miscarriage of justice** Oscar Slater was sentenced to death for the murder of Marian Gilchrist in 1909 but this was commuted to a life sentence. His advocates included Sherlock Holmes creator Sir Arthur Conan Doyle, who campaigned for his release. He was freed in 1927 and his conviction later quashed. He is pictured in Edinburgh with his US lawyers William Goodheart and Gordon Miller

▲ Dram fine mess A fireman attends a whisky spill from a road tanker. Lorry driver William Macfarlane had to scramble free

◄ Gangs in the gardens The Queensberry rules are forgotten in September 1971 as Radio One Club fans wade into each other with fists and feet in Princes Street Gardens

Destruction Aftermath of a gas explosion at a tenement in Guthrie Street in October 1989. Two people were killed by the blast

▲ **On guard** At the gates of Saughton Prison in the 60s

▲ **Dark past** The World's End Pub on the Royal Mile in January, 2001. Murder inquiry victims Helen Scott and Christine Eadie were last seen alive there in 1977

▶ **Wrecked** Bruntsfield House was damaged by fire in 1953. It has now been restored to its former glory and is one of the buildings that houses James Gillespie's High School

▶ **Notorious** The Prison Van Trial at the High Court in Edinburgh in 1922. A total of 13 alleged IRA members were tried for hijacking a police van in Glasgow's Rottenrow

▲ **Court appearance** One of 13 men accused of hijacking a prison van and killing a policeman leaves the High Court in Edinburgh in 1922. Six were found not guilty, the remaining seven, not proven

▼ **Blaze** Brown Bros & Co engineering works in McDonald Road, Broughton, in 1964

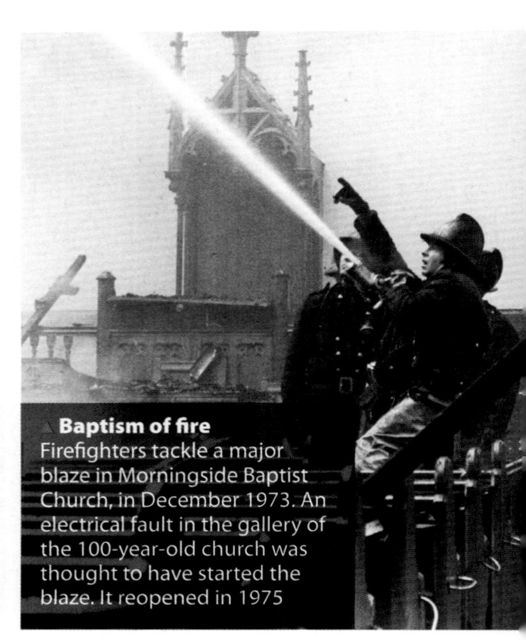

▲ **Baptism of fire** Firefighters tackle a major blaze in Morningside Baptist Church, in December 1973. An electrical fault in the gallery of the 100-year-old church was thought to have started the blaze. It reopened in 1975

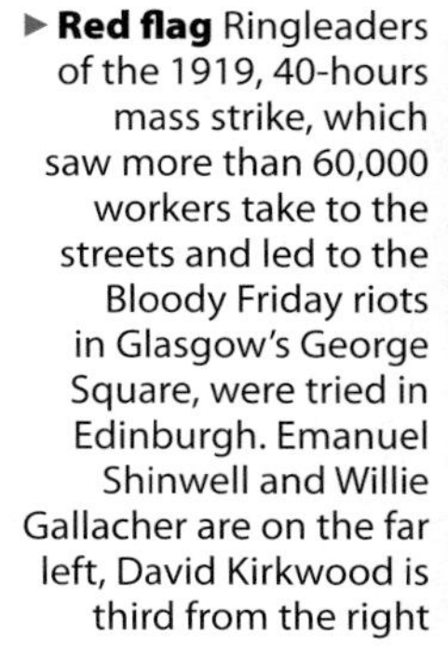

▸ **Red flag** Ringleaders of the 1919, 40-hours mass strike, which saw more than 60,000 workers take to the streets and led to the Bloody Friday riots in Glasgow's George Square, were tried in Edinburgh. Emanuel Shinwell and Willie Gallacher are on the far left, David Kirkwood is third from the right

◂ **Murder** The abandoned car which was to carry Major David Cunningham, Staff Sergeant Terence Hosker and Private John Thomson. They were murdered by fellow soldier Corporal Andrew Walker after they picked up a £19,000 payroll from a Penicuik bank to take it back to Glencorse Barracks, in January 1985. He was jailed for 27 years and freed from prison in 2011 on compassionate grounds

▴ **Colliery danger** A Mine Rescue Service team carry an injured miner on to their ambulance

City that boasts celebrity culture

Edinburgh, with its many festivals, has always attracted Hollywood's kings and queens

No entry
Actress Elizabeth Taylor and her husband Richard Burton walk away disappointed after not being allowed to enter Edinburgh Castle on July 22, 1963.

WILLIAM Shakespeare wrote that all the world's a stage – and much the same could also be said about Edinburgh.

From international personalities such as Danny Kaye, the world's highest paid actor and comedian in the 50s and 60s, to Rudolf Nureyev, arguably the world's greatest ballet dancer, to our own homegrown stars, they've all trooped through Edinburgh.

Back in the more innocent days, when the paparazzi didn't lurk around every corner, even the most famous of Hollywood's finest could walk around the capital – unaccompanied by PRs, assistants and entourages – just like any other tourist.

Nor did their fame grant them any special privileges.

If Richard Burton and Elizabeth Taylor, then at the height of their tempestuous love affair, and seen visiting the castle in 1963, looked far from happy, it wasn't necessarily because they'd just enjoyed one of their notorious bust-ups. It was because they had arrived after the official closing time and had been refused admission.

Meanwhile, real royalty, as opposed to Hollywood's Kings and Queens, from the starriest royal of them all, the late Princess Diana to its lesser members, have always been frequent visitors to the city, for both formal and informal occasions.

The Queen Mother's helicopter was regularly seen landing in Holyrood Park and, of course, the Queen and Prince Philip have spent a week in the palace in June ever since she came to the throne.

The corgis, until security was tightened up, used to be walked on Arthur's Seat, usually by a footman but occasionally by the royals themselves.

The International Arts Festival in August has always attracted the culture vultures but Edinburgh has equally happily hosted other less arty events including, in 1972, the Eurovison Song Contest – Luxembourg won and the UK's New Seekers came second.

Those were the days.

The Beatles appeared at the capital's ABC Cinema in 1964 and almost caused a riot, although Edinburgh's very own boy band of the 70s, the tartan bedecked Bay City Rollers – Eric Faulkner, Stuart Wood, Les McKeown and Alan Longmuir – were briefly the most famous group in the country.

Sean Connery, born in the city and known to his school friends and family as plain Tommy, was a milkman with the Co-op around the corner from his home in Fountainbridge until he uttered the immortal words, "The name's Bond, James Bond," and the rest is history.

Not that Connery is the only actor to have had a less than glittering start to their career.

Robbie Coltrane had, in his early days, a very special connection with Edinburgh. Before he went on to star in the BBC series Tutti Frutti in the 80s in his baggy tartan suit, he refused to accept what he deemed to be mediocre roles and worked instead on building sites.

He was responsible for replacing the elaborate chimney pots in the historic Milnes Court on the Royal Mile in the 70s. When he got the job, he asked what happened to the last guy and was told he'd fallen off.

The actor said: "They put a rope around my middle and tied the other end to the next chimney, which is set in. It was thought a bit jessie because, in those days, nobody bothered with hard hats or health and safety."

Good to know he trained for his role as Hagrid in Harry Potter on the rooftops of Edinburgh.

▶ **Waiting game**
Scotland team rugby stars Peter Stagg and Jim Telfer wait at Turnhouse for the plane to take them to Dublin for an international against Ireland in February 1970

▲ **Fab Four come to town**
The Beatles before their performance at the ABC Cinema in October 1964

Take that Legendary boxer Ken Buchanan pretending to spar with American singer Andy Williams

Home comfort aeme Souness, en 17, in Edinburgh th MP Tam Dalyell. ter leaving ttenham tspur and turning to inburgh due to mesickness, Dalyell ok up his case to released from contract after urs threatened to spend him from aying football for o years

Mum's the word The ueen Mother pictured on October 22, 1966, with Lord Provost of Edinburgh, Herbert Brechin, during her tour of the new James Gillespie's High School for girls

▼ Premium Bond
A young Sean Connery keeps himself fit while reading a script in 1957

► Film friends
Michael Caine and Sean Connery face the press at the Caledonian Hotel for the Edinburgh Film Festival in August 1997

▲ Royal visit
Princess Diana is pictured with the then Lord Provost Norman Irons as she attends an HIV conference at Heriot Watt University in 1993

▼ Taking steps
Andy Stewart, performing at the King's Theatre, is pictured arm in arm with dancing girls from the White Heather group

▼ Danny's gi
American actor and comedian Dan
Kaye with polio sufferers Maure
Allan and Lorraine Duncan on a v
to the Walpole Hall, on May 14, 19

▲ **Sound fellows**
The Bay City Rollers in the capital in February 1975

▶ **In with a shout**
Fans of the Bay City Rollers screaming for their idols while they perform at Edinburgh Odeon

▶ **Laughter lines**
Robbie Coltrane during a stand-up routine in1987

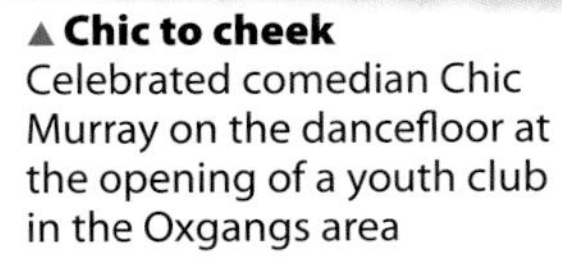

▲ **Chic to cheek**
Celebrated comedian Chic Murray on the dancefloor at the opening of a youth club in the Oxgangs area

▼ **Ballet high**
Rudolf Nureyev pictured at the Festival press conference on September 4, 1975

City of lights

Edinburgh has almost become firework city, with spectacular displays not only during the international festival but also at Hogmanay

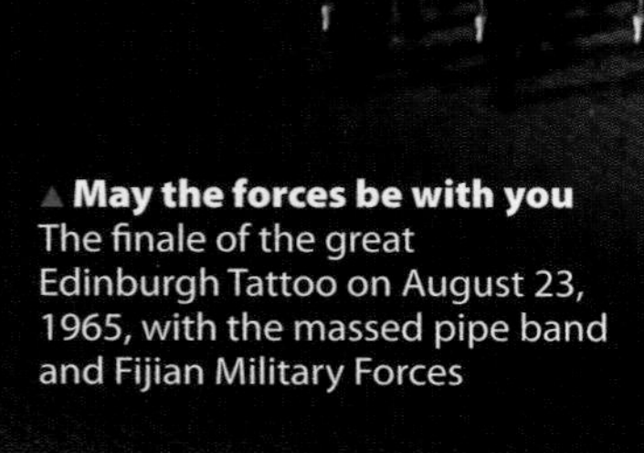

May the forces be with you The finale of the great Edinburgh Tattoo on August 23, 1965, with the massed pipe band and Fijian Military Forces

AT the last count, Edinburgh was home to 28 different festivals, including the Book Festival, the Film Festival and the Jazz Festival, of which you will have heard, and others such as iFest, the Scottish International Storytelling Festival, the Edinburgh's People's Festival and Edinburgh Annuale, of which you may not.

It is entirely possible that, by the time you have read this, there will very likely be a couple more.

They are all the children of the very first and still the grandaddy of them all, the Edinburgh International Festival of the Arts, dreamt up in 1947 in a very austere country recovering from World War II.

Its aim, its organisers said, was: "To provide a platform for the flowering of the human spirit."

Whether it succeeded is for its audiences to judge but, whatever else it did, it certainly provided a platform for all these other festivals, most but not all of which are crowded into August. The first was the Fringe, which right from the very start gatecrashed the official programme and eventually outgrew and overcame it.

Now it is the largest arts festival on Earth, with 2695 different shows in 279 different venues and with performers from theatrical greats, TV stars and famous or would-be famous comedians to students and amateur drama clubs from every single continent.

There is a myth that those who live in the city hate the festival and all its works and either shun the whole thing or leave Edinburgh altogether – only stopping to rent out their homes at exorbitant prices to the visitors who crowd into the Capital.

In fact, well over half the tickets are bought by natives and most of them enjoy the colour, fun and excitement the festivals bring.

The crowds who line Princes Street for the Festival Parade and who take advantage of the free performances on Fringe Sunday are proof of their popularity.

For the tourists, probably the must see is the Military Tattoo, which has been held on the forecourt of the Castle since 1950, with audiences perched high and a little perilously on temporary seats erected each year.

With the festivals have come fireworks.

Every night in August, they explode into the city sky, with the grande finale on the festival's last night. Then they are set to classical music, performed in the Ross Bandstand in Princes Street Gardens, while thousands watch.

More fireworks, too, at the city's Hogmanay celebrations, where the music is loud, raucous and mostly pop.

Edinburgh's dogs and cats it is said, don't come out from under the beds for months – and then, in this firework city to end all firework cities, it begins all over again.

▲ **He's a flier**
Alistair Mabbott, winner of the Edinburgh Festival Fringe 1982 poster competition, with his winning entry

▲ **Hot stuff**
The Edinburgh Festival Fringe cavalcade heads along Princes Street led by a massive dragon in August 2000

▶ **In the swing**
Canadian majorettes, performers at the Edinburgh Military Tattoo, liven up Princes Street in 1969

◀ **Steady does it**
A Hogmanay reveller heads home in the early hours after a richt guid nicht

▸ **Burning bright** Torchlight procession along Princes Street

▾ **It's a blast** A massive explosion of sound and colour at the Hogmanay event in Princes Street

▴ **Facing the music** Princes Street party revellers wearing masks and playing saxophones at the Hogmanay celebrations

▸ **The reel thing** Scottish soldiers perform Highland dance at the Festival

◂ **Not the real thing** Edinburgh Festival Fringe students in a show mimicking the Bay City Rollers pop group

▲ **Calling the tune**
Piper Elaine Marnach at the castle during the Edinburgh Military Tattoo in August 1977

▼ **Reined in**
Two-year-old Alayne Brown is led by her mother in the Edinburgh Festival parade

Where old meets new

The new Parliament, across the road from the Queen's official Scottish residence, Holyrood Palace, has heralded a new chapter in our capital's future

WE hope you have enjoyed this brief look at Edinburgh's history and the way in which the Capital and its residents have, over many centuries, evolved and grown.

From a relatively small town huddled around the castle, it has expanded north, south, east and west over the seven hills on which it is built – especially to the east, down to Leith.

Between 1833 and 1920, it was not only Edinburgh's port but an independent burgh – and many of its inhabitants still regard it as apart from Edinburgh rather than a part of the Capital.

The old warehouses that used to store cargo brought in from all around the world, have been turned into homes. Modern apartment blocks have been built around the dock area.

Here, too, the Scottish Government have their extensive executive offices that house the civil service – down at Victoria Quay.

It is at Leith that the Royal Yacht Britannia now lies at anchor, no longer a floating palace for the Queen but just another tourist attraction, where visitors can walk the same decks as the royals and their guests.

Like the yacht, Edinburgh has had its highs and its lows.

The flowering in the 18th century of what was known as "the Enlightenment" turned Edinburgh into one of Europe's great intellectual centres, just as the creation of the New Town made it an architectural gem.

It witnessed the growth of its successful financial sector but also saw the shine knocked off it after the crash of 2008, which so badly affected the reputations of the Bank of Scotland and its rival, the Royal Bank.

This of course is not the end of Edinburgh's story. There is the continuing saga of the new tram system, which has blocked off streets, diverted traffic and turned large parts of central Edinburgh into a gigantic building site since 2008. Initially, the trams were meant to run all the way from the airport down to Leith, but they will now stop in St Andrew Square.

The budget, originally £250million, has increased to more than £1billion while the time taken to build the system has also expanded. The projected date for the service to start has now moved from 2011 to 2014. Maybe.

Since the arrival of devolution in 1999, Edinburgh has become a capital city not only in name but as a seat of Government again.

Whether the referendum in 2014 will bring full independence and overturn the 170 Acts of Union is still to be decided.

But one thing is certain, Edinburgh will not stand still.